Birds of the North

Rachel Griffiths and Margaret Clyne

CELEBRATION PRESS
Pearson Learning Group

Map of the World

ARCTIC OCEAN

50°N

ATLANTIC OCEAN

NORTH AMERICA

CANADA

UNITED STATES OF AMERICA

SOUTH AMERICA

ALASKA

RUSSIAN FEDERATION

A S I A

EUROPE

UNITED KINGDOM

PACIFIC OCEAN

NEW ZEALAND

AUSTRALIA

INDIAN OCEAN

SOUTHERN OCEAN

Tropic of Cancer

AFRICA

Tropic of Capricorn

Equator

ATLANTIC OCEAN

Arctic Circle

Antarctic Circle

ANTARCTICA

N
E
S
W

0   1000   2000   3000   4000 miles

The Northern regions

Contents

Some species of birds, such as willow ptarmigan, inhabit the frigid climate of the far North.

Birds of the World

There are more than 9,700 **species** of birds found in the world today. Birds can be found on mountaintops and in valleys, in cities and on farmland, on lakes and rivers, in deserts and at sea.

Birds live in the driest, wettest, hottest, or coldest of places. Over time, birds have adapted to live in vastly different habitats.

Some birds are densely covered with thick feathers that **insulate** their bodies in cold climates. Many waterbirds have oily feathers that **repel** water, so that they keep dry. Some birds have webbed feet to help them swim. Birds that live in dry areas can go without water for long periods of time.

Most birds can fly. Flying helps a bird to move quickly from one place to another, to find food or shelter, or to escape **predators**.

The Feathers of Birds

Birds are the only feathered creatures in the world. Birds have four main types of feathers:

- small, contour, or outer layer feathers on the body that provide a streamlined covering;
- down feathers, under the body feathers, that keep the birds warm;
- flight feathers in the wings that tend to be unevenly shaped, long, and rigid;
- flight feathers in the tail that tend to be symmetrical, long, and rigid.

Birds have beaks of different shapes that enable them to find and eat different kinds of food.

The majestic bald eagle has a powerful, hooked beak that enables it to catch and eat live prey such as birds, small mammals, and fish.

Summer in the **tundra** brings flowers, fruits, and insects as food for birds of the North.

Birds of the North

Birds that live in the North, especially very far North, have adapted to living in extreme and harsh climates. Winters are long and cold. Snow covers the ground, and many lakes and rivers are frozen over. The days are short, and even when the sun shines, there is little warmth.

Summers of the North are short, but the days are long. When the snow and ice melt, plants begin to grow. They flower and produce fruit quickly before the cold sets in again. Insects that have survived the long, cold winter as eggs or pupae emerge and breed quickly. These insects provide food for the birds and, especially, for their young.

Birds of the North need food and shelter all year round. Some birds stay in the same area throughout the year and have adapted to the harsh climate. They are able to find food even when the ground is hard and covered with snow, and they are able to keep warm through the cold months.

Why Do Birds Migrate?

Many birds **migrate** in the winter to avoid the severe weather and to find food. Some move only short distances, from the mountains to the valleys, or to the coast. Some birds of the far North migrate to warmer countries far to the South in the winter. Others, like the Atlantic puffin, spend the winter at sea.

The Atlantic puffin spends the winter months at sea in the far North.

The Arctic loon

Arctic Loon

Loons are large diving birds with webbed feet and short wings. They are found in North America, Europe, and Asia. The Arctic loon is found across the north of Alaska, Canada, Europe, and Asia.

Loons are migratory birds. In winter, Arctic loons fly south to warmer areas and spend the winter months at sea. When the ice melts in spring, the loons return to northern freshwater lakes and pools for breeding.

The female builds a mound nest very near the water. She lays two long, glossy, spotted, dark-brown eggs. The eggs take about a month to hatch. As soon as the chicks hatch, they are able to swim.

The Arctic loon, which has a straight, thin bill, dives for food. In a single dive it can catch fish as well as **crustaceans**, **mollusks**, and worms. It uses its webbed feet and wings to move underwater.

Arctic Loon *(Gavia arctica)*

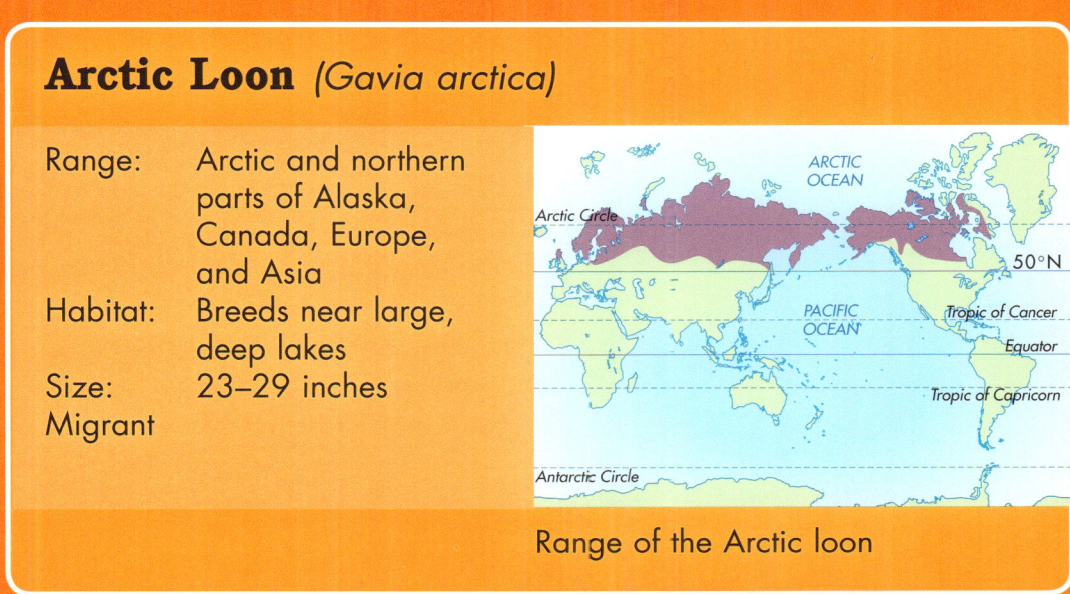

Range:	Arctic and northern parts of Alaska, Canada, Europe, and Asia
Habitat:	Breeds near large, deep lakes
Size:	23–29 inches
Migrant	

Range of the Arctic loon

The golden eagle is North America's largest predatory bird.

The Golden Eagle

The golden eagle is one of the largest birds of **prey** in the world. It has a wingspan of more than $6\frac{1}{2}$ feet. Its legs are covered with feathers to keep it warm.

Golden eagles live in mountains and forests across the Northern Hemisphere, including in the North of Asia, Europe, Africa, and North America. Many eagles of the North migrate south to lowland forests, wetlands, and rivers in winter. Others stay in the North all year round.

Golden eagles mate for life. A pair of eagles needs up to 56 miles of territory. They need such a large territory in order to find enough food.

Golden eagles hunt for small mammals, such as rabbits, hares, rats, and mice, as well as small reptiles.

They usually build a nest on a high cliff ledge, where they can get a good view of the surrounding country and watch for prey. Golden eagles, like other birds of prey, have very good eyesight.

Golden Eagle *(Aquila chrysaetos)*

Range: North America, Europe, Asia, and North Africa
Habitat: Breeds in mountains, moorlands, sea cliffs, and open upland forest
Size: 30–35 inches
Partial migrant

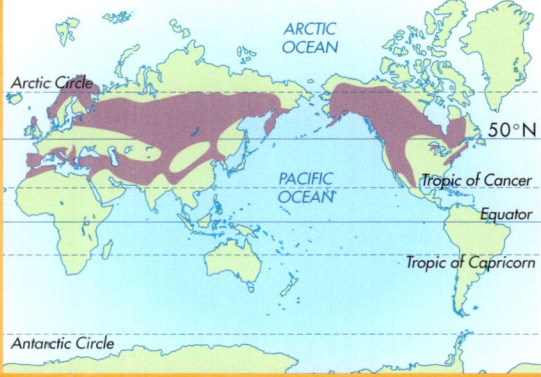

Range of the golden eagle

The willow ptarmigan

Willow Ptarmigan

The willow ptarmigan or grouse belongs to a family of three species of ptarmigan. Willow ptarmigans are found in the north of Europe, Asia, and North America. They stay in the North all year round.

Ptarmigans have short legs and feathers down to their toes. Most ptarmigans turn white in winter, and thus, are camouflaged or disguised in the snow.

Subspecies of Willow Ptarmigan

There are several subspecies of willow ptarmigan. The subspecies found in Scotland is the red grouse. Unlike other willow ptarmigans, the red grouse of Scotland do not turn white in winter.

In summer, willow ptarmigans eat a variety of plants and insects. In the autumn, as the insects disappear and plants stop growing, they migrate south from the high treeless tundra into the forests. They eat berries, seeds, and buds of flowers.

In winter, when the ground is covered in snow, willow ptarmigans eat buds and twigs from willow and birch trees. In spring, as the snow melts, they find insects, leaves and flowers. They also find berries that were hidden all winter under the snow.

Willow ptarmigan hens nest on the ground soon after the snow melts. They lay about six to ten eggs, which take three weeks to hatch. The male stays with the hen to look after the chicks. They are able to fly after ten days.

Willow Ptarmigan *(Lagopus lagopus)*

Range: Above 50° N in Europe, Asia, and North America
Habitat: Breeds in treeless tundra, moors, heaths, and Arctic willow bogs
Size: 15–17 inches
Partial migrant

Range of the willow ptarmigan

The Atlantic puffin

Atlantic Puffin

Puffins are small sea birds with black-and-white **plumage** and large, brightly-colored bills.

The Atlantic puffin is the only puffin found on the coasts of the Atlantic Ocean. Over time, they have adapted to swimming underwater. They can catch and hold several small fish in their beak at the same time.

Puffins do not fly as well as most other birds and have to work hard to take off into the air. When they land, they sometimes crash into and knock over other puffins that get in their way.

Atlantic puffins nest in burrows in the soft ground on grassy islands or at the tops of cliffs. The burrows can be up to 10 feet long. The female lays only one egg. Both parents **incubate** the egg. One parent incubates the egg during the day and the other at night. The egg takes about six weeks to hatch.

After hatching, the young bird remains in the burrow for about six weeks. The parents feed it whole fish.

Puffins spend the winter months at sea.

Atlantic Puffin (Fratercula arctica)

Range:	North Atlantic, Arctic Ocean
Habitat:	Nests in colonies on rocky coasts and offshore grassy islands
Size:	11–12 inches
Migrant	

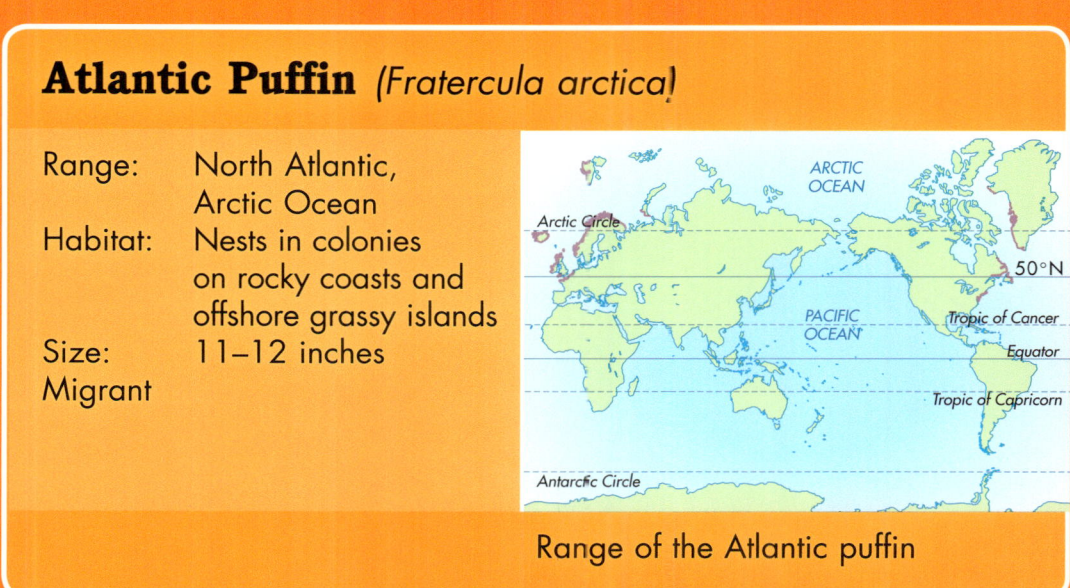

Range of the Atlantic puffin

The female snowy owl, with owlet

Snowy Owl

The snowy owl is a very large bird with mainly white feathers, yellow eyes, and a black bill. It is completely covered from beak to toe with thick feathers, which keep it warm in the coldest winter.

Snowy owls live mainly in the Arctic tundra and the grasslands of northern Europe, Asia, and North America. In winter, some stay in the Arctic, others move south.

The snowy owl usually nests on the ground, where there is no snow and where the owl has a good view of its surroundings.

The female usually lays between five and eight eggs, which hatch in just under five weeks. The young leave the nest well before they can fly. The parents continue to feed and look after them until they can fend for themselves.

Snowy owls hunt both by day and by night. They have excellent hearing and eyesight. They can swivel their head nearly all the way round. These three traits make it easy for them to find prey.

They hunt and catch small mammals such as lemmings, rats, mice, and hares; birds such as ptarmigan, ducks, and geese; and also fish.

Snowy Owl *(Nyctea scandiaca)*

Range: **Circumpolar** Arctic
Habitat: Breeds in Arctic tundra and Arctic **archipelago**
Size: 21–26 inches
Partial migrant

Range of the snowy owl

The Bohemian waxwing

Bohemian Waxwing

The Bohemian waxwing is found in the northern forests and woodlands of Europe, Asia, and North America. It is a small, pinkish brown bird with a crest, of tuft of feathers on its head, and "waxy" red-and-yellow markings on its wings and tail.

Waxwings eat mainly berries and other fruit and also insects. When food is scarce, or when the population grows too large, great flocks of waxwings move south and west to find better feeding grounds.

Bohemian Waxwings' Courtship

When looking for a mate, the male bird presents a berry, insect, or flower petal to the female. The birds pass the object back and forth from beak to beak, but neither bird ever swallows it.

Waxwings make a cup-shaped nest from grass, moss, pine needles, and other materials. They often nest high up in a tree. They lay between three and six pale blue-gray eggs that have black spots. They feed their young on insects.

Bohemian Waxwing *(Bombycilla garrulus)*

Range: Northern Europe, northern Asia, northwest Canada, and the United States
Habitat: Breeds in northern woodlands
Size: 7 inches
Partial migrant

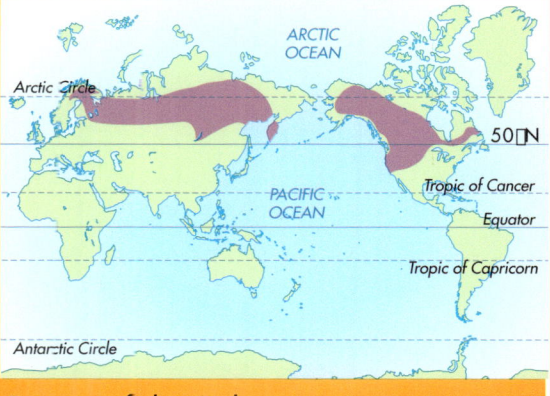

Range of the Bohemian waxwing

The Arctic tern   The willow warbler

Migration of Birds

Many birds migrate each year. Some birds of the North migrate long distances to warmer climates in the South to avoid the severe winter months. In summer, when insects are plentiful, they return to the North to breed. Two such birds are the Arctic tern and the willow warbler.

The Arctic tern spends the summer on the northern islands and coasts of North America, Asia, and Europe. When winter sets in, it flies up to 11,000 miles to the extreme regions of the Pacific and Atlantic Oceans, near Antarctica, where it is summer. The round trip is up to 22,000 miles.

The willow warbler is a small bird that breeds in Europe and in Siberia. It migrates to Central Africa to avoid the winter, a round trip of up to 16,000 miles.

A Migratory Bird of the South

The short-tailed shearwater migrates from south to north. In the southern summer, it nests in sandy burrows in Australia. Then, it migrates north to Japan and the northern Pacific Ocean area for the northern summer.

The short-tailed shearwater

Arctic Tern
(Sterna paradisea)

Range: Antarctica and northern
           North America, Europe,
           and Asia
Habitat: Tundra, at sea
Size: 13–14 inches
Migrant

Willow Warbler
(Phylloscopus trochilus)

Range: Siberia and Northern
           Europe, winters in Africa
Habitat: Woodland
Size: 4 inches
Migrant

Arctic tern
Willow warbler
Short-tailed shearwater

Migration routes of the Arctic tern, willow warbler, and short-tailed shearwater

The Eskimo curlew

Birds in Danger

The numbers of some birds of the North are falling, and some birds are in danger of becoming extinct. Threats to the birds of the North include hunting, loss of habitat, poisoning, and pollution. Some migrating birds are threatened in other parts of the world where they spend the winter or where they may stop to rest during their migration journey.

The Eskimo curlew is a critically endangered bird. There may be only fifty Eskimo curlews left in the world. This decline has been caused by excessive hunting in the nineteenth century and also the loss of grasslands in North America and South America, where these birds spend the winter.

Many countries are putting protection laws into place to ensure the future existence of the birds of the North.

DDT and Birds of Prey

The numbers of several birds of prey have fallen due to a chemical called DDT. This chemical was once widely used as an **insecticide** worldwide.

When birds of prey feed on animals that have eaten food sprayed with DDT, these birds also take in the insecticide. The effect DDT has is that it makes the shells of birds' eggs very thin, and the shells break before the chicks are ready to hatch. DDT has now been banned in most countries.

The bald eagle once suffered the effects of DDT but is now increasing in numbers.

Glossary

archipelago	a group of many islands
circumpolar	in the area around the North Pole or the South Pole
crustaceans	hard-shelled animals, such as shrimps, crabs, and lobsters
incubate	to keep eggs warm so that they hatch
insecticide	a spray used to kill insects, often sprayed on crops
insulate	to prevent heat from escaping
migrate	to move from one place to another
mollusks	soft-bodied animals, usually with shells, such as snails, mussels, and cuttlefish
plumage	the feathers covering a bird
predators	animals that hunt and kill other animals for food
prey	animals hunted for food
repel	to force back
species	groups or classes of animals or plants
tundra	vast, treeless plain of the far North

Index